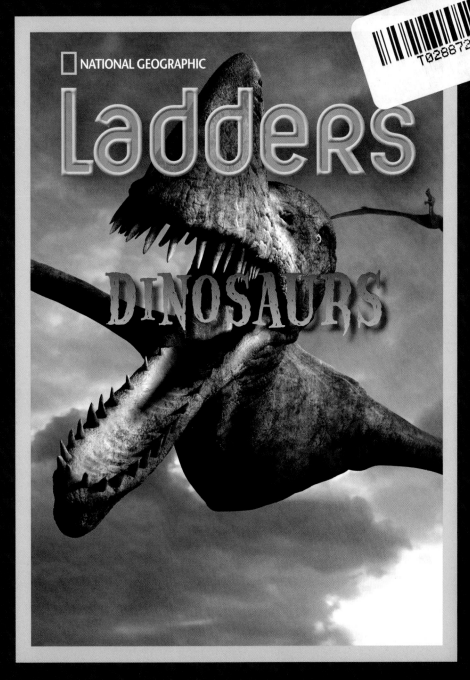

NATIONAL GEOGRAPHIC

Ladders

DINOSAURS

What Happened to the DINOSAURS?

by Allison K. Lim

illustrations by Ryan Durney

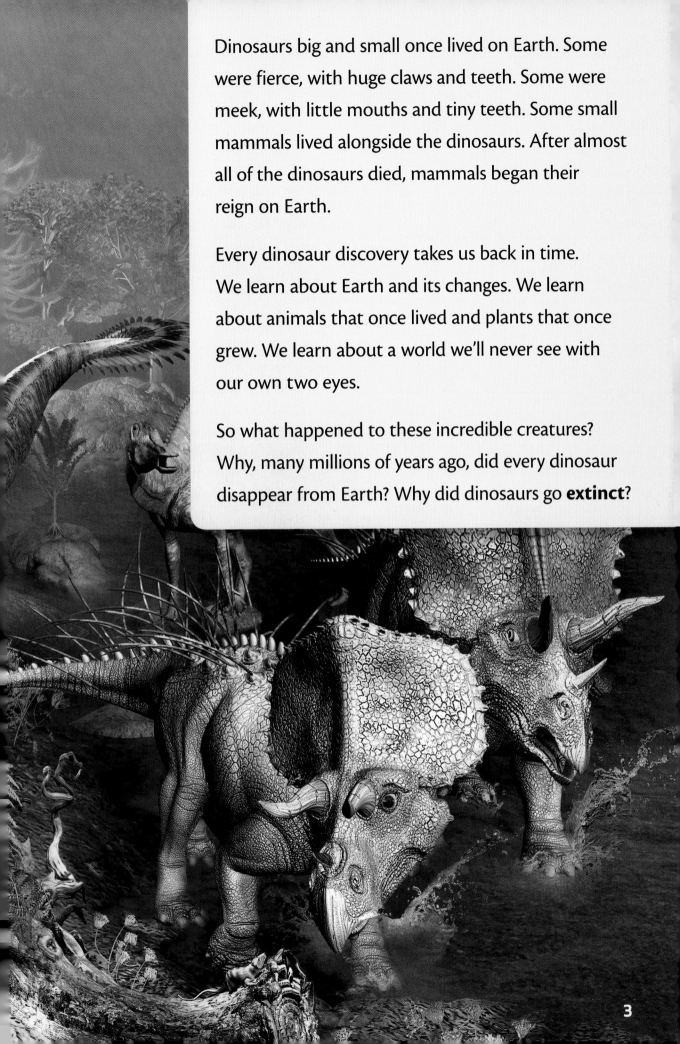

Dinosaurs big and small once lived on Earth. Some were fierce, with huge claws and teeth. Some were meek, with little mouths and tiny teeth. Some small mammals lived alongside the dinosaurs. After almost all of the dinosaurs died, mammals began their reign on Earth.

Every dinosaur discovery takes us back in time. We learn about Earth and its changes. We learn about animals that once lived and plants that once grew. We learn about a world we'll never see with our own two eyes.

So what happened to these incredible creatures? Why, many millions of years ago, did every dinosaur disappear from Earth? Why did dinosaurs go **extinct**?

Paleontologists often study soil and rock samples from a dig site. These samples can provide insight about where and when a dinosaur lived. As paleontologists study the samples, they may learn what Earth was like at the time the dinosaurs went extinct.

There are several ideas about what happened to the dinosaurs. Many scientists theorize, or think, Earth's climate changed very quickly. This caused temperatures to drop and water levels in the ocean to fall. Plants that were used to warm air couldn't adjust to cold air, and slowly began to die. The whole food chain was disrupted. **Herbivores** are animals that rely on plants for food. With fewer plants to eat, dinosaurs that were herbivores began to die from hunger. **Carnivores** that ate these herbivores died as well. Both **predator** and **prey** were in jeopardy. What's more, some scientists theorize that after this great chill, temperatures on Earth could have risen to an unbearable level for thousands of years.

Volcano Theory

A series of volcanic eruptions occurred in present-day India, lasting about one million years. The eruptions formed lava traps and most likely spewed ash, gas, and dust into the air. These events would have warmed and then cooled Earth considerably.

Asteroid Theory

An **asteroid** crashed to Earth, causing clouds of smoke and dust that blocked out sunlight for many months. Plants that depended on warm air and sunlight would have died.

Other Theories

Some scientists think insects infected the dinosaurs with diseases. Other scientists believe many factors created an environment in which dinosaurs and other animals could not have survived.

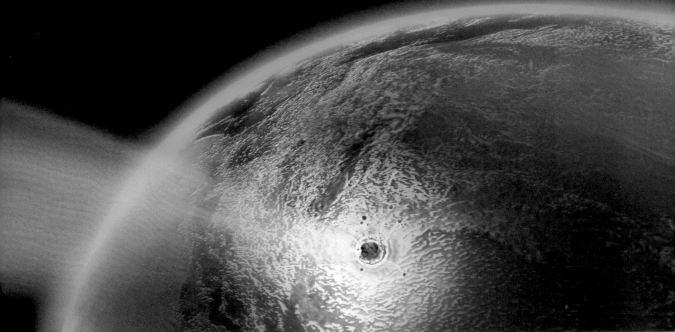

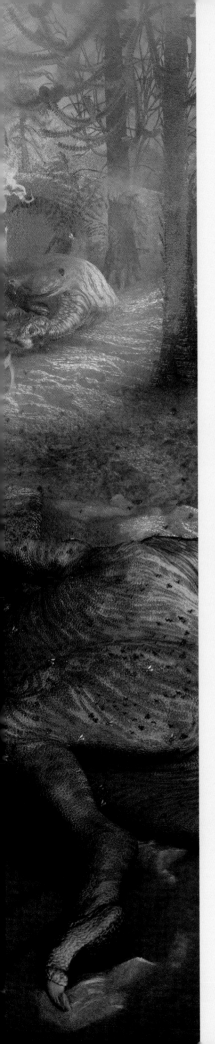

Although we may never know the exact reason the dinosaurs went extinct, many scientists think the asteroid theory makes the most sense. Much research supports this theory. Scientists know only a very large asteroid could have caused the extinction of dinosaurs. Such a large asteroid striking Earth would have caused a giant crater. A crater is a bowl-shaped hole in the ground caused by the impact of an asteroid.

Scientists studied rock samples from a crater along the coast of Mexico. This crater is more than 160 kilometers (100 miles) wide. The asteroid that crashed there must have been huge! The impact made an explosion that might have had lasting effects, including a change in Earth's climate. The rocks in the crater showed the asteroid struck at about the same time the dinosaurs went extinct.

What might have happened when this asteroid collided with Earth to form the crater? The huge explosion likely caused massive forest fires, tsunamis, earthquakes, and dust clouds that blocked sunlight from reaching Earth for several months.

Many plants and animals died, but many others survived. Scientists will continue to analyze rock and soil samples. In the meantime, the same question remains: What happened to the dinosaurs?

Check In What evidence supports the asteroid theory?

Digging Up the Past

with Rob Sula, Field Paleontologist

by Allison K. Lim | illustrations by Ryan Durney

Ranches in Nebraska
are good for hunting
fossils. This fossil was
an ancient tortoise.

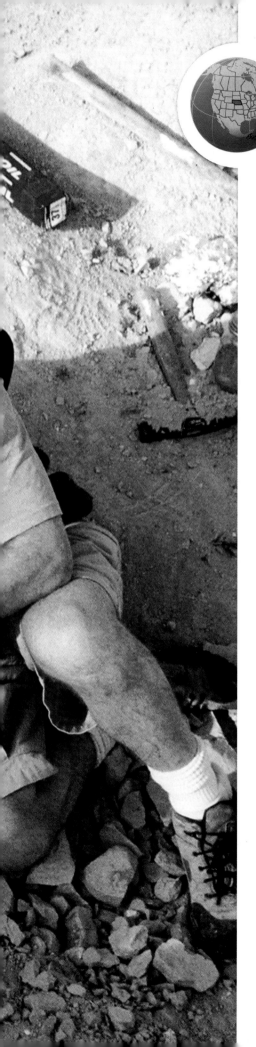

Fossil hunters, or field **paleontologists,** such as Rob Sula, certainly have interesting jobs. They search for hours, often under the hot sun, hoping to find buried treasure.

But finding "treasure" takes more than luck. Rob has to choose a location carefully and use his skills to determine if what he is seeing is rock or fossilized bone. Sometimes Rob goes home empty-handed. Other times, as in this story, he makes a great discovery.

What is now Nebraska was under a huge sea many millions of years ago. Plants and animals lived in the sea. Over time the sea dried up and the plants and animals perished. On many initial trips to Nebraska, Rob found fossils of small mammals. Then he heard there were large fossils at a nearby ranch. Knowing this area had once been covered by water, Rob suspected the fossils might belong to a sea creature called a **mosasaur.** He was right. The rancher led him right to a full mosasaur skeleton!

Rob was in awe! For the next few years, he searched on that same ranch. In 2003 he decided to explore an area of the ranch that was very isolated. There was no road to this area, so Rob had to hike to get there. But Rob thought this might be a good place to start looking.

At first, Rob found an unusual rock. Or was it a fossil? After careful examination, he discovered this was a fossil of a **vertebra,** or one part of a backbone. Rob knew it was common to find complete skeletons at this ranch, so he kept searching. He was hopeful that he might uncover the animal's full skeleton.

Here is the site as Rob found it, before the dig started.

After three hours of searching, Rob found another fossil. Then he found another. The fossils were articulated, or connected. Articulated fossils show an animal's bones connected in rock the same way they were connected when the animal was alive. Rob had soon unearthed six articulated tail vertebrae!

Rob, carefully preparing the fossils

Close-up of the tail fossil

The fossils were buried under layers of rock.

Three Kinds of Mosasaurs
(MOH-suh-SAWRS)

Rob studied the size and shape of the tail fossils. This was a mosasaur's tail. Mosasaurs were giant **reptiles** that swam in water. They lived at the same time as the dinosaurs and have been **extinct** for millions of years.

Tylosaur
(TIE-lo-SAWR)

Which kind of mosasaur did this tail belong to—a Platecarpus, a Tylosaur, or a Clidastes? There were slight differences in each of these animals' bones, but their skulls were drastically different. Rob had to find this animal's skull to know for sure to which kind of mosasaur these fossils belonged.

Rob studied the earth and the vertebrae for clues. Judging by the shape and direction of the vertebrae, he was nearing the end of the mosasaur's tail. Rob did not think he would find any other fossils from this mosasaur, so he stopped digging.

Platecarpus
(PLAT-ee-KAHR-puhs)

Clidastes
(klie-DAS-teez)

Rob stabilized the tail fossils by gluing them in place. Then he photographed them so he would remember exactly what the fossils looked like and how they were buried when he discovered them. Then Rob re-buried the fossils. He did this to protect the fragile fossils from wind and rain. They stayed buried for an entire year.

The next summer, Rob brought a team back to the site. They dug in the same location. They wanted to be sure they weren't leaving any remaining fossils behind.

First the team uncovered all of the fossils Rob had found the previous year. Then they continued to dig. They dug up another fossil of a vertebra, and then another. The fossils were from the same mosasaur!

Rob noticed teeth marks on the end of the tail bones. This observation was a key finding. Rob theorized a number of mosasaurs had died in one place and ancient sharks had eaten the tasty meat off their fleshy tails. That's why this mosasaur's tail was in an odd position. He was now hopeful he might find the rest of this mosasaur's skeleton.

Fossils of skin between the ribs

Fossils of ribs

Rob's team dug through 6 meters (20 feet) of soil and rock.

Fossil of skull

Rob's team was very excited and curious as to what else might lie ahead. The team unearthed one fossil after another. After hours of careful digging, the team reached the animal's rib cage. Upon careful inspection, Rob's team discovered something amazing. There was fossilized skin underneath the animal's ribs!

Finding a fossil of an animal is rare, but most fossils are of bones and teeth. Fossilized skin is extremely rare. This fossil erased most of the questions paleontologists had about mosasaurs' skin. Although they don't know what color the skin was, they now know mosasaurs' skin had diamond-shaped patterning on it, similar to a modern snake's skin. The skin was also extremely smooth, which probably helped the animal glide through the water.

Rob wondered if he might find the animal's skull as well. He thought about what he knew about the three types of mosasaurs. At about 2.5 meters (8 feet) long, Clidastes was the smallest mosasaur. This mosasaur was much too large to be a Clidastes. So was it a Platecarpus or a Tylosaur? The team continued to dig. They soon found two perfect flippers and a skull that was more than 1.2 meters (4 feet) long! As soon as Rob saw it, he knew what he had discovered.

It was a Tylosaur! Tylosaurs lived at the same time as *Tyrannosaurus rex* and died alongside the dinosaurs during the mass extinction many millions of years ago. These **carnivores** were some of the largest reptiles in the sea. They lived in water and breathed air at the surface. Tylosaurs never went on land and wouldn't have been able to survive out of the water.

These sea monsters were fierce **predators.** Powerful tails helped them swim quickly. Flippers helped them steer through the water. Long, pointy snouts helped them find **prey.** A Tylosaur would open its double-hinged jaw, much like a snake, and swallow a large animal whole. A row of pointy teeth lined each side of its jaw, and two more rows lined the roof of its mouth. Once a Tylosaur grasped its prey in its powerful jaws, the helpless animal would have no escape.

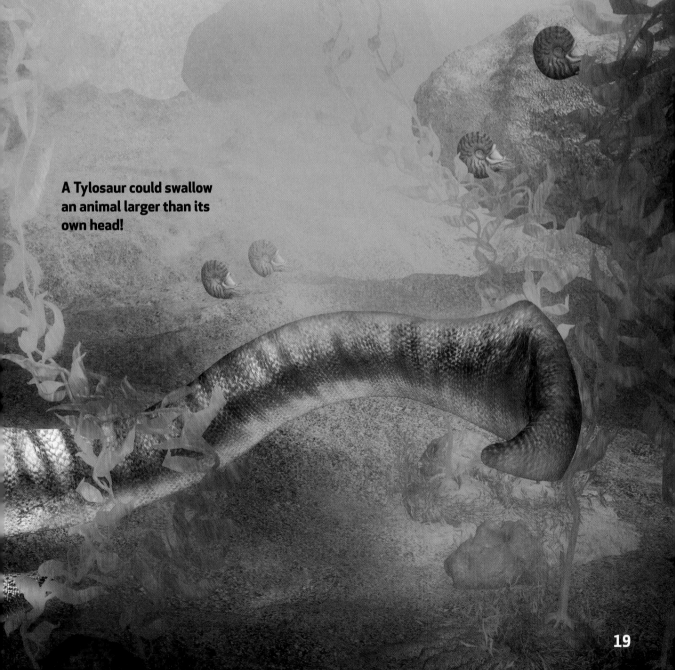

A Tylosaur could swallow an animal larger than its own head!

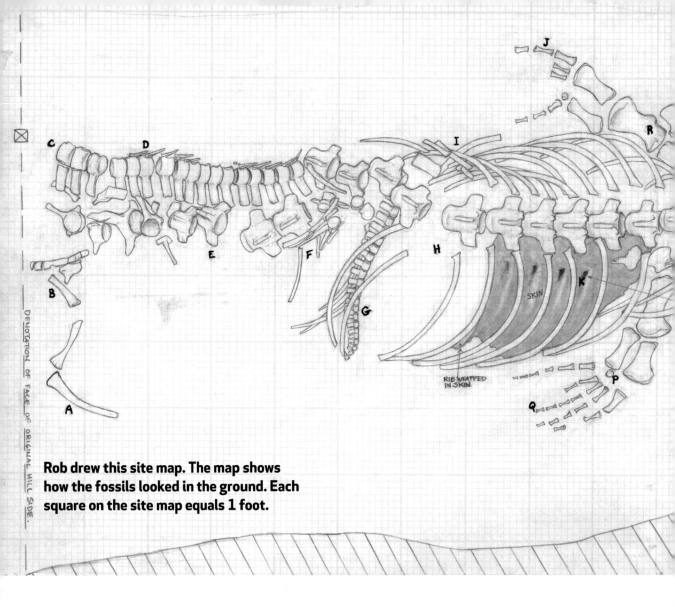

Labels on site map: C, D, J, I, R, B, E, F, H, K, SKIN, A, G, RIB WRAPPED IN SKIN, Q, P

DENOTATION OF FACE OF ORIGINAL HILL SIDE.

Rob drew this site map. The map shows how the fossils looked in the ground. Each square on the site map equals 1 foot.

Rob and his team had come across something incredible—a complete skeleton of a Tylosaur! Rob sketched drawings of the fossils on a site map, drawing each bone in its proper location. Field paleontologists like Rob create a site map so they can recall exactly how the bones were found in the earth. It also helps scientists piece the animal back together once the fossils make their way to the lab.

How paleontologists create a plaster jacket in the field:

1 Apply glue to the fossils. The glue hardens the fossils so they will not break when they are moved.

2 Dig a trench around the bones so the fossils and rock can be removed.

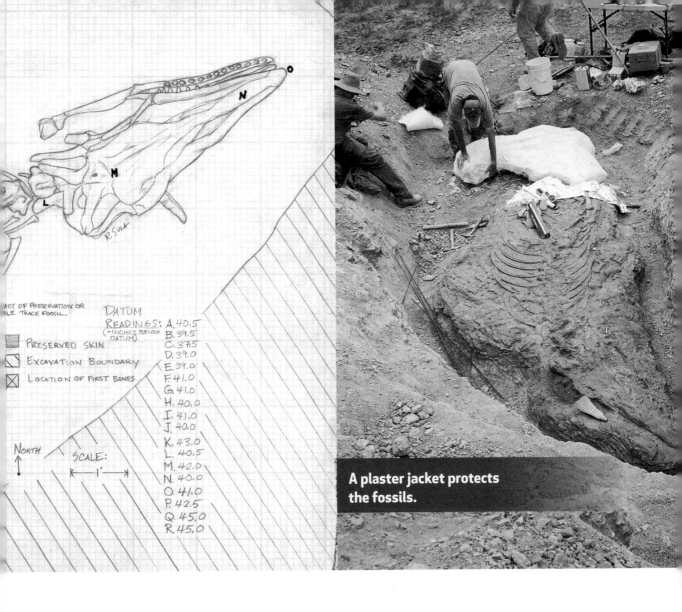

ACT OF PRESERVATION OR
BLE TRACE FOSSIL.

DATUM
READINGS: A. 40.5
(-INCHES BELOW   B. 39.5
DATUM)
C. 37.5
PRESERVED SKIN   D. 39.0
EXCAVATION BOUNDARY   E. 39.0
LOCATION OF FIRST BONES F. 41.0
G. 41.0
H. 40.0
I. 41.0
J. 40.0
K. 43.0
NORTH   L. 40.5
SCALE: M. 42.0
1'   N. 40.0
O. 41.0
P. 42.5
Q. 45.0
R. 45.0

R. SULA

A plaster jacket protects the fossils.

This Tylosaur had been buried for about 80 million years. Its fossils were brittle and extremely fragile. Rob knew it was his job to get the fossils back to the lab safely, so his team made plaster jackets to protect their amazing discovery.

3 Cover the fossils and rock with aluminum foil. Wrap the foil with duct tape.

4 Cover the wrapped fossils in a fiberglass mat coated with plaster. Use metal rods to reinforce the jacket.

5 Roll the jacket over. Wrap the other side.

Machines carefully move the fossils.

Once the fossils were secure inside their plaster jackets, Rob labeled each jacket on the site map. This would help paleontologists in the lab know which fossils to work on first. The team then transported the protected fossils to the lab.

Paleontologists in the lab are now preparing the fossils for a museum. They have finished removing the plaster and cleaning the Tylosaur's skull. They're taking their time on the rib cage though. They want to be sure they preserve as much of the Tylosaur's delicate skin as possible. We do not yet know where the Tylosaur will be displayed. We'll have to wait and see!

Check In What was special about Rob's Tylosaur fossil?

EXTREME DINOSAURS

by Allison K. Lim

illustrations by
Pixeldust Studios

Dinosaurs went **extinct** many millions
of years ago, so to study a dinosaur we
have to jump back in time. We do that by
unraveling clues held in rock for millions of
years. These clues are fossils. Some fossils
are more ordinary than others. Some are
downright astonishing. The dinosaurs on
these pages are some of the most extreme
dinosaurs discovered.

EXTREME TEETH

Adapted from *Extreme Dinosaurs,*
National Geographic Magazine, December 2007

MASIAKASAURUS

Masiakasaurus lived 70–65 million years ago. This fast-moving **carnivore** liked to feast on fish and other small animals. *Masiakasaurus* had a long neck and tail, but its most extreme feature was its teeth. **Paleontologists** think it used its hooked front teeth as a weapon to stab its **prey**.

Masiakasaurus fossil

EPIDENDROSAURUS

Epidendrosaurus lived 160 million years ago. Scientists think this 6-inch long tree-climber was an **omnivore,** meaning it ate plants and meat. It had three fingers on each of its two hands, but one finger was longer than the other two combined. Why did this small dinosaur have such a long third finger? It's a mystery!

EXTREME FINGERS

The size of a sparrow, *Epidendrosaurus* is the smallest dinosaur ever discovered. It most likely ate insects and berries.

Aye-Aye

Paleontologists often study a living animal for possible clues about a dinosaur. In this case, paleontologists study the aye-aye, a lemur that lives in Madagascar. The aye-aye and *Epidendrosaurus* might not be related, but they have the same puzzling body part. The aye-aye uses its long finger as a tool to pull grubs and insects out of holes in trees. It's possible *Epidendrosaurus* used its long finger in a similar way.

Epidendrosaurus fossil

After discovering these fossils in Mongolia, scientists are left asking questions. Was this an adult or a young *Epidendrosaurus*?

27

EXTREME SPINES

AMARGASAURUS

Amargasaurus lived 130–125 million years ago. This **herbivore** had two rows of spines on its neck and its back. Scientists have devised theories to explain the purpose of this dinosaur's impressive double spine, but they're still uncertain.

Compared with the size of its body, which was about 9–12 meters (30–40 feet) long, *Amargasaurus* had a tiny head. Scientists think this gentle giant was not very intelligent because small heads often contain small brains.

Amargasaurus might have had a skin-covered sail like some lizards alive today. It could have flushed blood into the sail to help cool itself down. But scientists aren't certain they've cracked the case. *Amargasaurus* could have also used its double spine to attract mates or scare off **predators**.

Amargasaurus fossil

At about 6 meters (20 feet) long and a little over 1.8 meters (6 feet) tall, *Tuojiangosaurus* used its strong tail to strike predators that tried to attack it.

TUOJIANGOSAURUS

Tuojiangosaurus lived 161–155 million years ago. This impressive herbivore had bony plates on its back and sharp spikes on its shoulders and tail. Scientists study dinosaurs that lived before *Tuojiangosaurus* to understand why this dinosaur needed back plates. Their sole purpose might have been to make *Tuojiangosaurus* look larger and more intimidating.

EXTREME SPIKES

Tuojiangosaurus fossil

STYRACOSAURUS

Styracosaurus lived 75 million years ago. While its ancestors had small nose bumps and frills on their skulls, *Styracosaurus* had a massive horn and frill. Measuring about 75 centimeters (2 feet, 6 inches), its nose horn was a deadly weapon. It likely used its horn to fight predators. Some scientists think the frill on its head could have changed color to attract mates or to make itself look intimidating.

Styracosaurus was the size of a rhinoceros.

& HORNS

Check In How might extreme features have helped these dinosaurs stay alive?

Discuss   Main Ideas

1. What do you think connects the three pieces that you read in this book? What makes you think that?

2. What is the main idea of "What Happened to the Dinosaurs?" Which theory do you think makes the most sense? Explain why.

3. Use Rob Sula's site map on pages 20–21 to tell about the mosasaur.

4. Which dinosaur do you think had the most interesting extreme feature? Explain why.

5. What do you still wonder about the dinosaurs or mosasaurs? What research could you do to find out more?